Have You Met Betty?

Diary of a Bad, Bad Bookkeeper

A Cautionary Tale for Small Business Owners Everywhere

By E. T. Barton

Diary of a Bad, Bad Bookkeeper

Notice: You do not have the right to reprint or resell this book.

You may not give this report away, or sell it.

© Copyright 2012 – All Rights Reserved – E.T. Barton

www.OneHourBookkeeper.com

ALL RIGHTS RESERVED.

DISCLAIMER AND / OR LEGAL NOTICES:

The information represented herein represents the views of the authors as of the date of publication. Because of the rate of which industry conditions change, the authors reserve the right to alter and update this publication and later publications based on new conditions. This publication is for informational purposes only.

While every attempt has been made to verify the information provided in this publication, neither the authors nor their affiliates and/or partners assume any responsibility for errors, inaccuracies or omissions. If legal advice or other related advice is needed, the services of a fully qualified professional should be sought.

Any reference to any person or business whether living or dead is purely coincidental.

Other Products by E.T. Barton or the OneHourBookkeeper.com website:

THE ONE HOUR BOOKKEEPING METHOD:

How To Do Your Books In One Hour Or Less

HOW TO START A LUCRATIVE VIRTUAL BOOKKEEPING BUSINESS:

A Step-by-Step Guide to Working Less and Making More in the Bookkeeping Industry

HOW TO DO A YEAR'S WORTH OF BOOKKEEPING IN ONE DAY

A Step-by-Step Guide for Small Businesses

Diary of a Bad, Bad Bookkeeper

10 WAYS TO SAVE MONEY ON BOOKKEEPING & ACCOUNTING

DIARY OF A BAD, BAD BOOKKEEPER

A Cautionary Embezzlement Tale

for Small Business Owners Everywhere

HOW TO TWITTER ON AUTO-PILOT

An Internet Marketing Guide for

Business Owners and Entrepreneurs

Diary of a Bad, Bad Bookkeeper

Diary of a Bad, Bad Bookkeeper

Diary of a Bad, Bad Bookkeeper

Table of Contents

Diary of a Bad, Bad Bookkeeper – (Day 1) A New Job 12

    Are You Hiring a Bad Bookkeeper? Listen for the Magic Phrase 13

Diary of a Bad, Bad Bookkeeper – (Day 9) In the Clear 16

    The Importance Behind the Bank Statement: 17

Diary of a Bad, Bad Bookkeeper (Day 14) – The Carnage Begins 18

    To Stop The Carnage Caused by Forgery: 19

Diary of a Bad, Bad Bookkeeper (Day 30) – The Double Payday Scam .. 21

    How to Catch the Double Payday Scam: 22

Diary of a Bad, Bad Bookkeeper (Day 40) – Stealing the Boss's Identity 23

    How to Prevent Identity Theft: 25

Diary of a Bad, Bad Bookkeeper (Day 55) – The Sister Company Scam . 27

    How to STOP the Sister Company Scam: 29

Diary of a Bad, Bad Bookkeeper: (Day 72) Bank Balance? What Bank Balance? 31

    What Any Business Owner Has the Right to Expect From Their Bookkeeper: 33

Diary of a Bad, Bad Bookkeeper

Diary of a Bad, Bad Bookkeeper: (Day 80) – The PayPal Weak Link and the Phishing Scam..35

   Stopping the Phishing Scam and the PayPal Weak Link:......................36

Diary of a Bad, Bad Bookkeeper – (Day 97) The Shell Company Scam ..40

   A Little More Information About Shell Company Scams: 42

Diary of a Bad, Bad Bookkeeper (Day 112) – Theft by Signature Stamp.45

   How to CATCH Theft-By-Signature Stamp: 48

Diary of a Bad, Bad Bookkeeper (Day 127) – The Payroll Tax Scam 50

   To Stop The Payroll Tax Scam:..52

Diary of a Bad, Bad Bookkeeper: (Day 140) – The C.O.D. Warning Sign 54

   Why C.O.D.'s are Warning Signs...57

Diary of a Bad, Bad Bookkeeper: (Day 149) The Collusion Scam 61

   How to Stop the Collusion Scam:...63

Diary of a Bad, Bad Bookkeeper (Day 195) – The IRS 65

   Keeping a Clean Bill of Health with the IRS...66

Diary of a Bad, Bad Bookkeeper: (Day 200) - Why the Accountant Did NOT Catch Me 69

   Why the Accountant Did NOT Catch the Embezzlement 70

Diary of a Bad, Bad Bookkeeper: (Day 216) - Men Suck!.........................73

   Why Skipping Vacations is a Warning Sign...76

Diary of a Not-So-Bad, Somewhat-Honest, "Better-Than-Betty" Bookkeeper: (Day 7) – Oh Crap! What do I do?..82

    Beginning the Audit Process..84

Diary of a Bad, Bad Bookkeeper

Diary of a Bad, Bad Bookkeeper

Diary of a Bad, Bad Bookkeeper

Diary of a Bad, Bad Bookkeeper – (Day 1) A New Job

Dear Diary,

I just started my new job today, and it's perfect. It's a small company with only a few employees, most of whom are never in the office – they all work "in the field." Also, there's a receptionist, so I won't have to be constantly answering the phone (thank goodness for that). The receptionist is very friendly, and I can tell that she's looking forward to having another woman in the office. Most of the other employees are men – all the better for what I have planned.

The interview went well (…of course it always does). The owner told me that he's never in the office because he's a contractor and he always has to be at a job site. He told me that I would have to "take initiative" and "put out a lot of fires." Basically, he wants to not have to deal with customers and vendors too much, and so he expects me to handle everything. Just as long as he's left out of it. *Idiot.* Still, it will make my job even easier.

Diary of a Bad, Bad Bookkeeper

I came in this morning and saw the owner just before he left. He handed me a set of keys for the office and told me where the checkbook was. He then showed me my office and stayed for a few minutes to chat. He told me that he had called a few of my references and he was satisfied. Thank heavens that the law won't let previous managers give bad references, lest they get sued. But even if that wasn't the law, there was no way in hell I was going to put down my ex-boss as a real reference. Nope – a friend is good enough…

Guess I should get back to work. Gotta learn the ropes...before I rob them blind.

Are You Hiring a Bad Bookkeeper? Listen for the Magic Phrase

Here's something I've always felt was a little scary about the court system in the United States:

Employers can no longer give a bad reference for their employees.

Well, they *can*, but for most states, giving a bad reference opens up the employer (or ex-employer) to a potential lawsuit. If someone doesn't get a job because of a bad reference, they have an actionable lawsuit against the offending party. How much does that suck for victims of a bad employee? As a business owner, you could have someone steal from you until you are on the brink of destruction, and yet you can't warn their next employer. It doesn't seem fair.

Well guess what... there *is* a warning sign that you're about to hire a bad employee. It's a ***Magic Phrase*** that once you hear it, you should let it ring the alarm bells in your head.

Are you ready for it?

Here it comes...

The Magic Phrase is, "**(Insert Name Here) worked here from (set date) to (set date). That's all I can say.**"

Let me rephrase that in a more understandable fashion.

"Betty Bookkeeper worked here from January to December of 2011. That's all I can say."

Why is that a magic phrase? Simple. Employers today are terrified of giving a bad reference in case the employee comes back and sues them, but they are *not* afraid to give a good reference. If you call an ex-employer and ask them to give a reference, you will either get a glowing review or the Magic Phrase.

Here's something else to think about:

Most job applicants are *not* going to give you the name of someone that will give them a bad reference. Instead, they will give you their friends' and relatives' phone numbers for references. If you have a resume in front of you for a potential employee, you should always consider tracking down the company's phone number and owner/boss of the applicant instead of just calling the person that is referred – unless the applicant is still working there, of course (since this could get them fired). If you can't get through to the owner, or if the person is still working there and doesn't want you to call their work because they may get fired if the boss knows they are job hunting, then call the job they had before their current job. You can't get them fired from a job they no longer work at. Also, you can try getting ahold of the Human Resources (HR) person instead or an Office Manager. Usually the Office Manager / HR Person won't have a personal vendetta against the employee (which bosses sometimes have), but they are just as conscious of the law as the boss. They will either give a great reference, or the Magic Phrase.

Diary of a Bad, Bad Bookkeeper – (Day 9) In the Clear

Dear Diary,

Well, it's been a little over a week and I would say I've got "the lay of the land." Apparently, the Owner wasn't kidding when he said he'd be out of the office a lot. I have yet to actually see him in the office for more than an hour a day. He comes into the office in the morning to give his field guys their daily assignments, then he talks to me for about 10 minutes before he too heads out. Right before he walks through the door, he stops and talks to the receptionist, telling her to forward all his important calls and take messages on the less important ones. Yada yada yada. Every day is the same (which bodes well for me.)

Today though was a really good day. Since the first day I got here, I've been the sole person in charge of the mail. And that mail comes to me unopened. Today, the bank statement came in. I've been waiting to see if the owner would make an exception when it comes to the bank statement, but he just tosses it on my desk without even looking at it. That's a good sign for me. That means when I start forging checks, he'll never know. Any checks that come back, I can shred before he gets them.

Man, I love working for "really busy" Small Business Owners.

The Importance Behind the Bank Statement:

To many, choosing the person that opens the bank statement is unimportant.

But here's the General Rule: ***He who opens the Bank Statement First is the One Who Can Steal the Most without Getting Caught.***

That means, if it's the bookkeeper – who has access to the checks – you are BEGGING them to steal from you. If it's the receptionist, that receptionist may end up in cahoots with your bookkeeper to steal from you. But if it's You-the-Small-Business-Owner, you can catch theft as soon as it happens. So be smart... open the bank statement first every time.

Even if you don't look for theft, opening the bank statement is often enough to dissuade embezzlers in your company before they get started.

Diary of a Bad, Bad Bookkeeper (Day 14) – The Carnage Begins

Well Diary,

Today was the day... the FIRST day that I stole from the company. Today, I forged my first check with the owner's signature. I would have done it a couple days ago – as soon as I found out the owner doesn't open the bank statements, and in fact expects me to do it – but the owner suddenly changed his pattern. Instead of staying out of the office, like he had done every day of the first nine days, he decided to stay in the office to "take care of some things." Since I wasn't expecting it, I decided to wait to see what it was he needed to take care of. Luckily, it wasn't anything that had to do with me or the books.

Well, even if it did have to do with the books, he wouldn't have found anything. I'm doing a very good job right now. After all, I have to prove my worth somehow.

I wrote the check for $100. I know, it's not much, but it's a start. Just something to see if he notices that I stole it. I'm sure he won't notice since I took the check out of sequence. But if he does, I can say it's for the Petty Cash Box that he doesn't have. If he doesn't notice... well then, I'm going to suggest he GET a Petty Cash Box. After all… "It makes MY job so much easier if we can have cash around for emergencies." (If this was a video, then right now is where I would do the evil laugh…)

And there are no worries about the bank clearing it. Banks don't have enough time to check every signature.

To Stop The Carnage Caused by Forgery:

Unfortunately, when a bookkeeper forges a check, the only way a Small Business Owner is going to know is if they open the bank statements first. And…the general rule is: He who opens the bank statement is the one who can hide or destroy the checks. So if an SBO opens the bank statement, they will get a chance to find the forged check before it can mysteriously disappear.

When you do open the bank statement, check that all signatures are your signatures. Take a second look at anything that was signed by a signature stamp or doesn't look like your signature. Also, look for check numbers that are obviously way out of sequence or missing a check number because there's a good possibility that it's a forged check.

If your bookkeeper did cash a forged check, contact your bank and inform them that the check was forged. Sometimes, they will be able to pull the funds from whatever bank account they were deposited in and put those funds back in your account. But – more than likely – once the check has cleared, you can't get the money back. So be vigilant in opening the bank statement BEFORE your bookkeeper does.

Diary of a Bad, Bad Bookkeeper (Day 30) – The Double Payday Scam

Dear Diary,

Today was payday – the second since I've been here. I figured it was about time to test the Double Payday Scam – to see if my boss would actually catch me.

So, I started the day by doing the Payroll. Just like two weeks ago, I created and took all of the paychecks to the boss to sign. He signed them, with only the occasional request to see a corresponding timecard…then he signed mine without question.

I took the checks back to my office and set mine aside. Then, I printed up another paycheck that I took back to him.

"What's this?" he asked me, glancing briefly at my double payday.

"It's a replacement check. I double-checked my income and realized that I had entered my withholdings incorrectly, and QuickBooks took out too much in taxes. So I voided the other one and reprinted this one."

"Okay," he said, shrugging and then signing my check.

And just like that – Double payday. If he had asked me to produce the voided check, I would have gone back to my office and voided the first check... but since he didn't, he'll never know. Even if he opens the bank statement (which let's face it, he probably won't), he'll see the extra paycheck and think he's just looked at the same check twice.

How to Catch the Double Payday Scam:

All a small business owner has to do to catch the Double Payday Scam is to ask to see the voided check, or to insist that you will void all checks personally. They can then re-file the checks, and you have protected yourself... it's that simple...

Diary of a Bad, Bad Bookkeeper (Day 40) – Stealing the Boss's Identity

Dear Diary,

I got a new credit card today. Well, technically, I got a new "company credit card" today. When the boss wasn't around, I went ahead and called his credit card company and told them we had lost his company card and needed a new one. They asked me for all of the usual identifying information – social security number, mother's maiden name, address, phone, account number, etc. – and of course, I gave the guy on the other end of the line all of that information. I then told him that I wanted to change the password question "because the last bookkeeper got fired, and we need to protect my boss's identity."

The guy at the credit card company didn't even miss a beat – after all, companies get new bookkeepers all the time. "Which question would you like?" the guy asked me. "Do you want a question about your high school, pets, favorite cities…" and on and on and on.

"How about the question about pets," I answered innocently.

"Okay. What is your pet's name?" he asked.

I thought really quickly, and then answered, "Moron."

"Excuse me," the guy on the phone said.

"My pet's name is Moron," I repeated sincerely. What I wanted to add was – "and Moron's my boss" – but I managed to hold my tongue… barely. It was so hard.

"Okay. Moron it is," the guy said in a serious tone while clicking away at the keys on the other end of the phone. "Anything else I can help you with?"

"Oh. I almost forgot," I added. "Our office has moved. The address I gave you was for the old address. The new address and phone number is…" and then I gave him my home address and personal cell number.

Again, I heard clicking on the other end of the line as the poor dupe updated my boss's "new information." When he was done, he said, "You should get that credit card in the mail by…" which turned out was today.

So, I swung by my house and checked the mail during lunch. The card was already there. So I went ahead and treated myself to lunch – on the boss, of course. After all, he doesn't pay me nearly enough for all the excellent work I do for him. And since the boss never opens the mail – especially that particular credit card bill– what he doesn't know what hurt him.

I wonder what I'll buy tomorrow… Maybe some new earrings. I've always wanted pearls…

How to Prevent Identity Theft:

You would not believe how incredibly frustrating it is to call into your credit card company and find out that all of your password information has been changed. Not only can your password info be changed, but some people even go so far as to change the "mother's maiden name" question. Of course, the simplest way to stop this is to catch it early.

You can do so by doing the following:

Open your credit card statements, or check your transactions online regularly. If anything seems questionable – no matter how small or large – call the credit card company immediately and ask them how many cards they've sent out. You can also verify that your security information is still what you originally created.

If they tell you your password information has changed, be sure to throw a high holy conniption fit and demand to speak to an account manager or "their boss." Get this account closed immediately because whoever has your card can still make purchases even while you're on the line. They will send you a new credit card with a new credit card number within a matter of days.

Get copies of your three credit reports as soon as you possibly can because – quite frankly – if your private information has been changed, there's nothing to keep them from signing up for more credit cards at vendors you may never even have heard of. But, the good news is that every single one of those stolen cards will show up on your credit reports, but not always all three of the reports, which is why you should spend the extra money to access all three. (In fact, for $14.95 a month at Transunion, you can actually access those three reports and credit scores for free every month. It may be worth it if you ever find yourself a victim of identity fraud.)

If a credit card company calls you and says there is questionable activity on your account, get online immediately and see what they are talking about. If they are contacting you, they are probably seeing something they've never seen on your account before. So even if you have your credit card on you, it never hurts to double check whatever charges they're concerned about.

And lastly, make sure you know where ALL cards are at all times. I once had a client who ordered a card for his wife – a card which never arrived. It turned out, someone stole it from his mailbox and was shopping with it in the next town and my client never knew. Luckily, I caught it with the very next credit card statement when I asked for receipts that matched the charges, and we realized immediately what had happened. So even though the thief had managed to steal more than $7,000 in 15 short days, my client was not liable for a penny, especially because he disputed the charges right away (which is another good reason to check those statements every month.)

Diary of a Bad, Bad Bookkeeper (Day 55) – The Sister Company Scam

Dear Diary,

Today I became a business owner. That's right -- I've opened my own business and am about to make a million dollars the easy way – with little or no money down. Okay – I spent a little money. But technically, it wasn't my money. It was my boss's money – or maybe I should call him my "investor" – not that he knows he's an investor.

If only all those companies touting their "make a million dollars without doing any work at all" plans knew how easy it really was… because my way really is the "no work necessary" way.

Anyway… I went down to the courthouse today on my lunch break, a little bit of petty cash in hand. I registered a new "DBA," also known as a Fictitious Business Name. The form only cost $20 and now I have a business name. The lady behind the counter told me that I would have to run the new business name in the newspaper for 30 days to announce my new business venture, but it can be any newspaper in the county. I found a small newspaper company that will do it for about $25 for the whole month. Pretty good deal, huh?

So once I had my Fictitious Business Name document in hand, I went down to the bank and opened up a "business checking account" for $15 a month. I even went to the same bank as my boss's bank. Figured it means less driving around when I have to go the bank for him. And normally, I wouldn't pay so much for a checking account, but again, it's not my money.

So guess what my new company's name is…

Well, Diary, you know how I work for "Smith's Distribution Company". I named my company "Smith's Distinguished Corporation." The reason...stealing, of course. I've seen a lot of deposits come across my desk and I noticed a pattern on the checks. People tend to write the checks to "Smith's," "Smith's Dist.," or "Smith's Dist. Co." Seeing all those checks, I suddenly realized that I can totally steal those checks. Since "Smith's Distribution Company" is not fully printed on the check, I can put it into my new business checking account and the tellers will assume that the abbreviations on the checks are short for the name of my company. They'll probably even assume that the name of my company is just a sister company to my boss's business. And unless he goes down to the bank and asks if I have my own business checking account, there's no real way that he's going to know what I'm up too.

After work, I actually made my first deposit. It was a check for $1,200. See – the experts were right. You do have to spend money to make money. All I had to spend was $60 and I made my first $1,200. This is going to be sweeeeeet!

How to STOP the Sister Company Scam:

As mentioned above, it's nearly impossible to know if someone in your company has begun this scam. You would first have to guess the Sister Company's name as closely as possible before you can even look it up – although you can try and look it up at your local County Recorder's Office. Most likely, you won't find anything online about the Sister Company because the Embezzler would have to advertise their theft for it to show up in search engines… and there's no way they're going to admit to anyone but a diary that they're a scum-sucking thief.

Now, just because it's hard to spot the scam, doesn't mean it's hard to stop the scam. The reason this scam happens is because it's an easy "crime of opportunity." It gets by because no one thinks to double check it. To do this, all you have to do is get a "For Deposit Stamp" (or to put it another way, an Endorsement Stamp).

Think about this: When you go to a large retailer like Target, what do they do with checks? As soon as the cashier receives the check, they run it through the machine, and the machine prints an endorsement on the back. That prevents the check from going into any bank account but the one linked to that business. That's what a "Deposit Stamp" can do for you.

When you stamp a check on the back with your company name, account number, and the words "For Deposit Only," the bank will then make sure that check gets into the correct account. Period. It's that simple. You can also get a stamp for the front of the check that will stamp your company's full and accurate name, but the best way to prevent this kind of fraud is to get an Endorsement Stamp. This kind of custom stamp is often $10-$20 at online sites, but I found a deal to get a free stamp at www.iPrint.com – all you pay is shipping and handling. That's a $15 value for $3.49 S&H total. Check it out and get yours today if you don't already have one: www.OneHourBookkeeper.com/SignatureStamp.

Diary of a Bad, Bad Bookkeeper: (Day 72) Bank Balance? What Bank Balance?

Dear Diary,

Today, was a funny day. The boss came into my office, and he had this look on his face. It was a look like, I'm gonna get answers – no matter what.

Pasting an innocent expression on my face, I quickly hid the Mafia Wars game on my computer screen and turned my full attention to him. "What's up, Boss?" I asked.

"Hey, Betty. I was just wondering – how much money do we have in the checking account right now?"

Oh Crap, I thought. He's not catching on to me, is he? "Why do you ask?"

"Well, I was checking out the iPads online, and I was thinking I wanted to get one of the ones with 3G—"

Diary of a Bad, Bad Bookkeeper

You and Me both!

"—But I don't want to have to finance it. I figured maybe we could pay cash for it. So, I was just wondering what our bank balance was."

Heck if I know.

Okay, maybe I do know, but I can't tell him the real balance. "I'll have to get back to you on that one," I told him.

He looked around at the large piles of paperwork on my desk, his face twisting with irritation. "You can't just pull up some report and tell me?" It was obvious he didn't like my carefully gathered piles of paperwork, but I had to look busy.

"It's not that easy," I lied. "I have so much work, it's going to take me a while to get you an accurate balance."

"I can wait," he said, leaning against the table in my office.

It was then, I knew… I would have to pull out the big guns to get him to drop the subject.

Grabbing my stomach, I grunted and shifted in my seat.

"You okay?" he asked.

I waved a hand nonchalantly. "Oh, sure. I'm fine. It's just… I'm cramping. I'm PMS'ing right now, and my stomach is really hurting. I want to get you that balance, but I'm in so much pain."

He stiffened, as if I'd slapped him, and quickly came to his feet. Then, his face turned red so fast, I thought steam would shoot out of his ears.

"You're hurting that much?" he asked, inching toward the door.

I whimpered and nodded. I wanted to drive it home with a few tears – just to see if I could get sweat to break out on his balding forehead – but I've never been good at making myself cry. So instead, I did the whole wobbly chin thing.

"You know what – you're busy," he told me, from the hallway now. "I can get it another time. Just let me know the balance when you can." And with that, he turned on one heel and practically sprinted away.

I was hard-pressed not to start laughing out loud. But I realized a hard truth. Men will always run when it comes to PMS and tears.

I will definitely remember that next time.

What Any Business Owner Has the Right to Expect From Their Bookkeeper:

I know a lot of bookkeepers may get mad at me for saying this, but in my opinion, when a business owner asks "What is my bank balance?" the bookkeeper should be able to answer fairly quickly. A good bookkeeper will be doing the bank reconciliations regularly – as in, within a week of receiving the bank statements. And even if they don't have an exact balance because there are checks and debits outstanding, they should still be able to estimate fairly accurately what the current balance is. If they can't tell you the balance – or estimate it – or if they say it will take a couple days to do the bank reconciliation, take this as a warning sign. The Bank Register is one of the most important things a bookkeeper manages, and they should be on top of it. Personally, it has never taken me longer than an hour to do a Bank Reconciliation, and that's with entering checks. Obviously, give them time to calculate it, but it's reasonable to expect the balance by the end of the day.

Diary of a Bad, Bad Bookkeeper: (Day 80) – The PayPal Weak Link and the Phishing Scam

Dear Diary,

Today I got an intriguing email. The email was a confirmation from PayPal. It said that we had spent $150 on an online order. Since the company does not have a PayPal account, I knew it was a scam – a Phishing Scam, where some con artist is trying to get access to our account. When you click on the links in the email, you are taken to a fake PayPal page where you are encouraged to log in and verify the purchase (or deny it), and then the fake website captures your real log in details and the con artist can then empty out your PayPal account. Any good back office person knows – you never click on links in emails from financial websites (because it's easy to "cloak" the website links). You always go directly to the original website and log in there.

Obviously the PayPal notice was a con…but it got me thinking. Our company does not have a PayPal account…but we could. It only takes a few minutes to set up, and then you can make payments from any checking account or credit card account that you link to it.

So I opened one.

Then, I went online and made a purchase to Office Depot.

When I checked the bank balance online, I saw that the payment was debited as a PayPal account to Office Depot. As far as I'm concerned, the explanation from the bank is simple enough to satisfy the boss. Now, I don't need to forge checks unless I really want to.

Now the only question is…what should I buy?

Stopping the Phishing Scam and the PayPal Weak Link:

In this mini story, there are actually two cons I've brought up: The Phishing Scam and The PayPal Weak Link.

The Phishing Scam is an actual scam where a thief sends a fake email encouraging you to click on the link in the email. By doing so, they can capture your login information and then clean out your bank accounts. PayPal Emails are the most common financial cons. After PayPal, sending emails from banks would be the second most common way con artists get information from their victims.

There are three easy ways to spot these scams:

Banks and financial institutions have standard, precise emails already created that always use the same verbiage. Phishing emails, on the other hand, often have misspellings and/or sentences that don't make sense. If anything doesn't seem right with any financial institution's email, it probably isn't from your financial institution.

When you open the email, you will see the "From" address is not necessarily from the financial institution it claims to be from. Whatever is after the "@" sign is the website address. Anything in addition to the normal address probably means the email is a scam. (For example: …@paypal.fakesite.com or …@fakesite.paypal.alerts.com.) Both the paypal.fakesite.com and the fakesite.paypal.alerts.com are fake because whatever comes before the .com is the site. That means, these sites would be fakesite.com and alerts.com…not PayPal.com.

And finally, banks and financial institutions openly encourage customers to NOT click on links from their emails because Phishing Scams are so common. Instead, they will tell you to go directly to their actual website to log in so that you can verify if the email is from the bank or not (and thus the alert is fake or not).

Also, it's common to get emails from banks you don't even have an account with. If that happens, obviously you can ignore those…but if you are concerned that an embezzler has opened an account in your name, just print out that email and go down to the bank to see if you have an account or not.

AND when in doubt – go directly to the source…never click on the links in an email from a Financial Institution.

As for the second con – The PayPal Weak Link:

It is very, very easy to open a PayPal account and link it to a checking account…any checking account. PayPal has a very simple verification process, which means that creating a PayPal account is easy for anyone with access to your checking account information, including your bookkeeper. From there, it is very easy to steal money because PayPal and the bank account link together in order to create instant money transfers. Plus, money can be sent to anyone with another PayPal account, and everyone takes PayPal these days (including airlines and other travel agencies), so stealing becomes very easy.

Therefore, to protect yourself from someone linking a PayPal account to YOUR checking account, you need to link it first. In other words, you need to be the one to create a PayPal account with your checking account. PayPal only allows a checking account to be linked ONCE, which means no one else can use the checking account information. Once you have linked it, keep that information to yourself. There's no need to share it with your bookkeeper or anyone else because businesses should stick to using Bank Bill Pay and writing checks…Period. PayPal should only be used by one person…the creator of that account.

Thus, if you don't have a PayPal account, start one immediately in order to protect your checking account. If PayPal does NOT let you create a PayPal account, then an embezzler has already linked to your checking account, and you need to consider closing it. This is one of those huge companies that you just can't avoid, and you really shouldn't avoid.

Diary of a Bad, Bad Bookkeeper – (Day 97) The Shell Company Scam

Dear Diary,

Another day, another dollar…or at least, another stolen dollar.

Well – I've had my own company for about two weeks now and I've made a couple thousand dollars skimming off the deposits. The boss hasn't noticed. As far as he's concerned, all of the invoices are paid, and I'm doing my job incredibly well. In fact, I just passed the three month trial period, and the boss gave me a $0.50 an hour raise. When he told me that, I felt like saying, "Really? A whole $0.50 an hour. You're too kind. Now I can buy that car I need." But instead, I didn't.

Still, I do need a new car. Fifty cents an hour is only an extra $1,040 per year. That's not even going to pay for a cup holder. My car is breaking down and dying in the most inconvenient places, so I really just want to get a new car. I don't really need anything fancy, but the best cars are at least $20,000. I need to figure out how to get a bigger down payment. I want to put down at least $5,000, but the way things are going, that's going to take a couple more weeks. I have no idea if my car can make it a couple more weeks.

I thought about starting another business, but I don't really want to pay another $100 or so for the licenses…plus, the time it takes to go to the bank and get another account…I'd rather not.

But I did come up with another idea. I wrote a check to Johnson Hauling for $1,500.

"What's this check for," the boss asked me when I gave it to him to sign. I had been hoping he wouldn't notice it, since I slipped it in with a bunch of other checks. But since he had…

"That's a new vendor we're using," I told him. "We needed to haul away a bunch of left over trash and remnants from the newest renovation project, and they were the best deal. They delivered a trash can to the project, then hauled it away when they were done."

In case I didn't mention it, the company I work for buys, renovates and sells houses. So paying $1,500 to haul away remnants was not that uncommon.

"Okay," he said, distracted as he signed the next check, and then the next. Finally, he handed me the pile of checks and gave me a dismissive wave of his hand.

I left the office triumphant. The truth was, I didn't need to create another company because Johnson Hauling is my husband's company. The check that he had just written, I was able to cash at the bank because I'm a signer on the Johnson Hauling bank account. My husband will never know that I got this money because I can just cash the check. And the boss has never met my husband, so he has no idea that my husband and I have different last names. The result... I am now $1,500 closer to buying my new car.

I think I'll go test drive a Toyota Prius. It's a very energy efficient car. After all, it's my moral duty to save the planet.

A Little More Information About Shell Company Scams:

This scam is commonly referred to as a shell company scam because the embezzler is paying a valid company for services that were never rendered or products that were never delivered. Thus, the company is solid with a banking history while the transaction is nothing but air. Any teller will cash that check without qualms and hand over the money to whomever's name is on the account.

This scam is also often pulled when a payment is made to an individual or an employee. The embezzler's excuse might be that this person was just a subcontractor for the day and was paid under the table. Many times, the embezzler will even go so far as to pay someone they are friends with, and then let the friend take a portion of the embezzled funds.

They can steal for a long time this way without getting caught, especially because the owner gets used to seeing that name.

To Stop This Scam:

It's important to do your homework. If you don't recognize the name of a company, or know anything about the transaction that took place, then ask questions – lots of questions. Ask who ordered the product or services. Whoever requested the order – sometimes it might be another employee – it's important to ask them why they placed that order. Ask to see a Purchase Order, Shipping Receipt, or an Invoice from the company. Go and look at the service that was done or the product that was delivered. Talk to someone at the company for which the check is written too and make sure that they actually delivered the product or service. A good rule of thumb is this… If the payment is for a new account – whether a vendor, employee, subcontractor, or customer – demand proof. Make contact, or ask for paperwork.

Warning Signs:

If someone is colluding with the embezzler to steal from you, they may look you straight in the eye and lie about what they've done for your company. That's why it's important to go with your gut when you meet someone. If you don't like them, "fire them."

Also, if you ask for paperwork and it doesn't have an address or phone number, be suspicious. Valid companies automatically put their contact information on all their paperwork because they want to make sure they get paid – and if you can't call them with questions, you won't be paying. So, ask for the invoice or statement, and be very, very slow at paying anyone you're suspicious of. Let them call you and demand payment when in doubt.

Diary of a Bad, Bad Bookkeeper (Day 112) – Theft by Signature Stamp

Dear Diary,

Today the boss went on vacation and guess what he gave me…the Signature Stamp. I couldn't believe it when he handed it to me. I think my smile was from ear-to-ear. Doesn't he realize how stupid it is to give me the signature stamp?

"Are you sure you want to give this to me?" I asked all innocent like. In the back of my mind, I was already calculating how much money I might be able to get now that I had this new stamp.

"Of course. I trust you," he told me with an amused little smirk.

That smirk told me everything I needed to know. My question had just convinced him that I was the sweet innocent young lady he had come to know so well. Because – fool that he was – he sincerely believed that everyone was as open and honest as he was.

I almost felt bad about stealing from him. Almost. But then I would remember that I was making less money than everyone else in his company…everyone except the receptionist.

"I don't know. That's a lot of responsibility," I commented in the best hemming-and-hawing voice I could manage. "I really don't want to let you down."

"It'll be fine," he assured me with a light pat on my shoulder.

Then he strolled out of my office. An hour later, he left the office for good. He was off to the Caribbean for the next two weeks.

I waited an hour after he left just to make sure he wasn't coming back.

And then…

Over the next week…

I signed some IRS paperwork with that signature stamp. Whether or not the IRS paperwork is accurate…? Who cares. At least it's filed.

I opened a new cell phone account with his signature stamp…got the "Unlimited Text and Talk" package…for my whole family. My daughter may only be 8, but she loves her pretty new pink cell phone. And of course, I love my new iPhone.

I also got a new Business Gas Card Account.

I downloaded a new bank account application from online, signed it with his signature stamp and faxed the paperwork back . Got instant approval.

Diary of a Bad, Bad Bookkeeper

I sent out several applications to local vendors to get lines of credit. They all got approved. I now own a chainsaw from the local hardware store (because I can), an electric lawnmower from Lowes, solar panels for the garden from the local garden supply store, and $300 window blinds from Home Depot.

I ordered a bunch of magazine subscriptions in his name and sent them to my house. (I really love Cosmo.)

I walked into Office Depot and paid for a whole bunch of office supplies with a blank company check and his signature…including a new printer for my kids and a portable scanner for… I guess for the "heck of it."

I went to the bank with a check made out to Cash. (That was an easy $500.)

I paid my new car's DMV bills with his check…and got my husband's car smogged.

I signed a few petitions in his name. He's now a Democrat that actively supports breast cancer funding.

I also got a PO Box in his name at the local Mailboxes Etc. office. All that new paperwork will never even come to the office.

…And I did a whole bunch of other stuff, although I can't remember them at the moment.

You know what the best thing is, Diary? When he comes back, he'll have no idea what I've done. Most of the paperwork will go to the new

PO Box I opened in his name. And even if he comes back and asks to see the bank statement for the first time ever, he still won't know what I've done. I can explain away the DMV and car-related bills as "work needed on one of the company vehicles," the Office Depot check as "supplies we needed" and the Cash check as "Petty Cash" issues that came up. All the rest...well... there's just no way he can find out about that stuff. At least none that I can see.

How to CATCH Theft-By-Signature Stamp:

You can't.

You can't catch this kind of theft because you've given them a free pass to steal from you. And since your bookkeeper has access to all of your most personal information – social security numbers, DOBs, Tax ID Numbers – you've just made it super easy for them to take anything they want in your name. That means – YOU are responsible LEGALLY for EVERYTHING they've done. The IRS says you owe money, and they have your legal signature on file...then you have to pay it or try to fight it. It's your signature. And if you lose, you have to pay penalties and interest on top of the paperwork they've filed.

Okay – you CAN catch this kind of theft, but you'll need a professionals help after the fact to find out what that bad bookkeeper did.

Now you can PREVENT this kind of theft by NOT giving your signature stamp to anyone who has access to your checks, credit cards, or any kind of personal information. Maybe that person is your office manager or receptionist. Maybe you can give it to your accountant and make your bookkeeper go to them to get your signature. Either way, by adding a second person to the mix whenever you go on vacation, thus giving the second person you're signature stamp, you are taking steps to actively prevent embezzlement while you're away.

AND REMEMBER – IF YOU EVEN SUSPECT BOOKKEEPING FRAUD, ASK YOUR ACCOUNTANT FOR HELP. You're not crazy.

Diary of a Bad, Bad Bookkeeper (Day 127) – The Payroll Tax Scam

Dear Diary,

Today, I was bored at work. Really bored. I mean – surf-the-internet-looking-for-designer-handbags bored. (And I don't even like designer handbags…although I wouldn't mind a Brighton.)

Anyway…it was Payroll Day, which usually I'm happy about. When payroll comes around, I take my sweet time entering all the timecards and wages. I tell the boss it's an all-day project, but in actuality, I'm done before lunchtime. I usually bring the checks into his office around 4PM, thus I get the rest of the afternoon to screw around online.

So there I was, surfing Bag, Borrow or Steal, when the receptionist walked in. I quickly switched the windows on my computer to show the payroll. Ironically, it was my own check.

"When do you think the payroll checks will be ready?" the receptionist asked me.

Diary of a Bad, Bad Bookkeeper

"Why do you wanna know?" I asked in my most annoyed voice.

She inched toward the door, clearly uncomfortable by my unwelcoming persona. "It's just, I have to leave at lunchtime, and I'm going on vacation for the weekend. I was kinda hoping to get that check before I left."

"Oh. Well then, I'll put a rush on your paycheck," I told her.

Her little ears actually turned pink with pleasure as she thanked me effusively and scooched out of my office.

That was when I turned my attention back to the monitor and realized something. I had inadvertently changed my Federal tax deduction amount from $200 to $0. I don't think I'd ever realized before that it was so easy to change the payroll taxes before cutting a check.

It was my Ah-Ha moment – like Oprah always talks about. I realized in that moment, I could zero out my taxes to get more money with every paycheck, but then still pay the regular tax amount to the IRS each and every payday. Then, at the end of the year, I could file my taxes and get a BIG-FAT refund. Even better, I could make my boss overpay the taxes on everyone every week and file the paperwork at the end of the year declaring that all of those excessive taxes were deducted from my paychecks alone, and then get an even larger refund. If I could manage to make the weekly payroll amounts the same every payday, the boss wouldn't think to look twice at the money being deducted from the account.

The question now is: how much can I get away with paying before the boss notices a difference?

To Stop The Payroll Tax Scam:

This is one of the sneakiest types of embezzlement, especially because it's common for an employer to pay a lot of money in payroll taxes. Also, it's common for bookkeepers to adjust individual government taxes for each pay period because usually, it's only the individual employee who would have to face the consequences – that of dealing with the IRS at the end of the year and trying to get a refund or make up the difference. The biggest embezzlement possibility happens when the final paperwork is filed at the end of the year – the paperwork that details out who paid what in employee/employer taxes. It is on that paperwork where an embezzler can declare that they overpaid in their taxes and thus deserved to get ALL of that money back.

Therefore, to catch and prevent this kind of embezzlement, you need to:

1. Look closely at the individual taxes of the person who creates the paychecks. (This should be on an attached paystub.) Compare it to someone who makes approximately the same amount during that

period. Look to see if the tax amounts are very different or only slightly skewed. A big difference will either mean that the two individuals claim different deductions during the year, or that the tax numbers were overridden.

2. Periodically, add up the individual taxes for all of the employees being paid. Once you have a total tally, compare it to the payment that was made to the government. (You should see this on the bank statement or credit card statement that was used to make the taxes.) If the totals are not the same, then you definitely have a problem. That problem could be embezzlement, or it could just be that your bookkeeper is dyslexic.

3. Finally, have someone other than the person entering the payroll fill out the final payroll tax paperwork at the end of the year. Even though it will cost you more to pay an accountant to do this, it could potentially save you thousands in overpaid taxes that an embezzler will claim as a refund. All you have to do is send a copy of your bookkeeping file to your accountant, and then your accountant can take a closer look at anything that doesn't look right.

If you have any other suggestions on how to stop this type of embezzlement, please share it. The only way to stop embezzlers from destroying the companies they work with, is through educating each other about how they're getting away with it.

Diary of a Bad, Bad Bookkeeper: (Day 140) – The C.O.D. Warning Sign

Dear Diary,

Today sucked… and I mean, straight up sucked.

There I was, minding my own business, when in walks the boss with a receipt. On the receipt are stamped the letters C.O.D. It was from one of our vendors that apparently hasn't been paid in so long, they've changed our account from credit to C.O.D.

"What is this, Betty?" the boss asked me. "Why has ABC Hardware turned our credit account into a Cash-on-Delivery account? I've been with them for five years, and they're saying we're three months behind in our payments. I told Bill – the boss over there – that it can't be right. We've never missed a payment with them, but their bookkeeper swears we're late. What's going on?"

I looked at him as innocently as I could, and shrugged. "It has to be a mistake, Boss. I'm certain we're current."

Diary of a Bad, Bad Bookkeeper

"Can you call them and fix this, please?"

"Sure. No problem."

Then, the boss practically tosses the bill at me and storms out of my office.

I picked up the phone line, figuring he'd probably be watching the extension from his office to make sure I called, but I didn't bother dialing the number right away. I knew the truth – we were behind. I should have made that payment a while ago, but I knew if I sent it, the checking account would go in the hole. Since I wasn't quite sure how far behind we were, I figured I'd better check.

Typing a few things into the computer, I saw that we were about $1,200 behind. That wasn't too bad. So I did actually call the bookkeeper over at ABC Hardware. When she got on the phone, I said, "Hey, Jane. How's it going?"

"Betty," she said coldly.

A few choice words ran through my head, but of course I kept them to myself. "Listen, Jane. I just got reamed by my boss about some notice he got from your company. He said you made our account a C.O.D. account. What's up with that?"

"Well, Betty, you're company is late in paying us. And it's not the first time."

"Well, Jane... I just mailed a check for $1,200 a couple days ago. Have you checked your mail today?"

"'The check's in the mail?' Really, Betty? You've used that one before. And then we never got the check. So my boss decided to make your account C.O.D. from now on. Besides, you owe us $3,100 – not $1,200."

No kidding. "Are you sure about that? I only have invoices for $1,200."

"I'm sure. In fact, I emailed you and faxed you hard copies of the invoices several times over the last couple months."

The temptation to hang up on her was irresistible, but I didn't. "Well, I'm sorry, but I don't know what happened to the invoices. And I did send you $1,200 just a couple days ago. So, what's it going to take to forget this whole C.O.D. thing?"

"If you want the account to revert back to a credit account, you need to pay the balance in full immediately. That's the only way."

"Okay. I can do that. I'll put a check in the mail today."

"No, that's alright. I'll come and pick it up."

Of course you will, you snotty... "Okie dokie. How about five o' clock? I can have a check for you by then." And the boss will be gone by four, so he'll never see the real balance due.

"Fine, see you at five." Then, she actually hung up on me.

Long story short, I had to scramble and figure out a way to pay $3,100 without letting the boss know what was going on. It took me a bit, but I finally figured out that I could write a balance transfer check from one of the new credit cards I opened in the company's name...a credit card that goes to the Company P.O. Box the boss doesn't know about.

I told the boss it was just a misunderstanding, and that Jane actually found our payment in the mail that day...so there should be no problem from now on. The boss went back to thinking I'm a genius, and Jane showed up at 4:45 – Eager twit.

All I have to say now is: Man, that was a close call!

Why C.O.D.'s are Warning Signs

A lot of small business owners don't realize it, but when a credit account is changed to a C.O.D. account, that's usually a BIG warning sign that "the business is suffering". (Notice, I'm NOT saying anyone's embezzling...this is quite simply a sign that the business needs to handle their finances better, and possibly their cash better as well.) Most vendors that offer credit to their preferred clients are loathe to take that line of credit away if it means they might lose a business as a customer. Usually, the only reason a vendor would change a credit account is if there is a history of serious delinquency or bounced checks. So the minute any vendor demands a COD payment, realize that your company's credit history is on shaky ground and become proactive.

How to Know for Sure

Should the above scenario happen to your company, don't go running to your bookkeeper first. Instead, ask the bookkeeper at your vendor's company to print up a Statement of at least 90 days to 6 months so that you have a record of EXACTLY how your bookkeeper has been paying them. Look it over and take note of how far apart the payments are. Are there any amounts that were subtracted and added back on? (That could be the sign of a bounced check.) Most credit accounts require a minimum of one payment a month, while some require more. Ask the other bookkeeper what the terms are for your company, and THEN approach your bookkeeper.

Before you make any accusations, however, there is one more thing you can do to double check your bookkeeper. When you have the Vendor's Statement for your company in hand, ask your bookkeeper for the last three bank statements. Also, ask for a "Check Detail" listing all of the checks for the same three months. A good bookkeeper will know exactly where those bank statements are and will be able to give you both documents in less than 10 minutes. (The key is to ask for this information immediately and DO NOT let your bookkeeper put you off 'til the end of the day...they can cover their tracks if given too much time.) Then, when you have the Vendor Statement, the Check Detail, and the Bank Statements in your hand, do a quick check for the following:

Highlight the check numbers listed on your Vendor Statement.

Find the corresponding check numbers on your Check Detail printout. From here, you will be able to tell exactly when the check was supposed to have been printed and then mailed. The dates should be a week apart if the vendor is in town...up to 10 days if the vendor. (Of course, the time it takes to cash a check also depends on how big the vendor is.)

Now check the bank statements for the same check numbers. Do the dollar amounts actually match, and when were the checks cashed? Sometimes, the other company may hold onto the check for any number of reasons, but it will give you a good idea of how long the check cashing process takes with THAT particular vendor...and how long your bookkeeper may be holding checks.

Your Bookkeeper May Be Embezzling if...

Now, before I tell you exactly what to look for as far as embezzling goes, let me just say one thing. This does NOT 100% mean that your bookkeeper is embezzling. There can be reasons for any discrepancies you find. However, if you do find the following discrepancies, don't be stupid and sit on your hands either. Ask an accountant or an independent bookkeeping company for help immediately. Make a backup of your bookkeeping program without the bookkeeper's knowledge, and put that aside...(you may need it later).

And whatever else you do... DO NOT...I repeat... DO NOT confront your bookkeeper with what you find. If your bookkeeper IS an embezzler, the MINUTE you accuse them of anything, they will WIPE their hard drive, and your bookkeeping program, and they will destroy any evidence of embezzlement you may have in your office. Be certain first, and then do a cold hard lockout. The minute you KNOW – without a doubt – that they're embezzling, DO NOT let them back in the office, and disconnect the bookkeeping computer from the internet. (You don't want them logging on remotely to destroy your bookkeeping program.)

To know if your bookkeeper might be embezzling, look at the Check Run and look at the Bank Statements. Do the check numbers and amounts match? Bookkeepers can always go in and change the check names and amounts later on (which they will do if they want to show the boss an inflated bank balance), but the Bank Statements will give them away every time.

Another thing to pay attention to…are the checks being cashed months after they were written? If they are, then your bookkeeper was sitting on them for some reason (probably to make sure they didn't bounce)…but keep in mind, YOU may have told your bookkeeper to hold those checks. That happens a lot, so don't make any accusations unless you're sure you did NOT ask the checks to be held.

Again, this is just a warning sign, but it's a good sign to look for. Do not ignore it.

Diary of a Bad, Bad Bookkeeper: (Day 149) The Collusion Scam

Dear Diary,

Today was a not-so-great day. Apparently, I have a partner now. I never intended to have a partner, but it appears I have no choice in the matter. Here's what happened:

I was in my office (innocently shredding checks), when I suddenly heard a man say, "I know what you're doing."

Quickly slipping the leftover checks back into my desk drawer, I looked at him with my most innocent expression. "What do you mean?" I asked sweetly. It was Ernie, one of the flooring installers that handled the bigger clients. He was considered the boss's second-hand man. "What do you think I'm doing?"

"You're destroying the evidence."

Crap. How did he know? But I decided to play it cool. "What evidence?" I scoffed. "I don't know what you're talking about."

"Those checks you're shredding are the checks you've forged. Am I right?"

"Why would you say that?" I demanded, pretending to be affronted.

"Because I've seen all the signs before. The new car…the fancy clothes. You order lunch all the time instead of bringing it from home like the rest of us." He glanced down the hall behind him, then stepped into my office, lowering his voice as he did. "I know what you're doing…and I want in."

In? Was he nuts? "I don't know what you're talking about."

"Yeah, you do. And you can either cut me in, or I'll rat you out."

Cold chills ran up and down my spine, and my palms were actually sweating. I could tell by the smug look on his face that he knew he had me between a rock and a hard place.

"Look," he continued, propping himself onto the edge of my desk and leaning toward me. "You don't have to tell me everything you're doing. I don't really care. I just want a piece of the action. And I have the perfect way to do it."

I narrowed my eyes. "Oh yeah. What's that?" I asked.

"Simple. I have a friend that runs his own construction company and can get us plenty of jobs. You cut some checks to his company with an additional amount of money, and he'll pay the rest of the money back to us. The boss won't ask questions because he'll be able to see that the work is getting done, and we can make a tidy sum on the side. So what do you say? Should I call my friend? Or should I call the boss?"

"The boss won't believe you. He trusts me 100%."

"He trusted his last bookkeeper too – until I accused her of a few things. And I've been here for seven years. Who do you think he's gonna believe?"

And just like that, I had a new partner. But at least if we're both stealing, he can't accuse me of anything without me making a few accusations back. I won't be going down alone if he decides to betray me.

On the plus side, it is a quid pro quo situation. I help him make a little extra money, and he gets me new carpeting in my entire house. I think I want purple…

How to Stop the Collusion Scam:

Spotting and stopping the Collusion Scam is really difficult. For one thing, the invoices that the bookkeeper receives will match the checks going out. That makes embezzlement even more difficult for an auditor (or auditing accountant) to find because there's legitimate backup and everything appears to be "on the up and up." For another thing, the money being paid out will not have your bookkeeper's name on it, and the money they'll be taking home will be coming from one or many of their colluding partners.

Therefore, to spot and stop this scam, you need to trust your gut. Pay attention to who is hanging out in your bookkeeper's office. Most bookkeeping positions involve staring at a computer all day, and if someone is spending more time than necessary or usual, take note. Begin observing that employee as well and see who they recommend as "work associates." Keep an eye out for how many checks they receive each month, and if those payments seem a bit high. Also, look for signs that those employees are spending more money than they're making. Oftentimes, an employee's spouse will make a lot more money than the employee, but there will be a consistent spending pattern if that is the case. It's the sudden changes you want to look for.

Also, since one of the easiest ways to stop embezzlement is to be the only person who opens bank statements as they come in, you want to keep an extra watchful eye out for checks to vendors or customers that also seem "a little too high." If you feel like a company is making too much money for various projects…shop around. Call that company's competitors and see what they would charge. And stay open to switching vendors. Because the truth is – you never know when someone is going to decide to steal from you…"by any means necessary."

Diary of a Bad, Bad Bookkeeper (Day 195) – The IRS

Dear Diary,

Today I got a notice from the IRS. Luckily, the receptionist passed the letter to me unopened before the boss saw it (she didn't know what it was), and he doesn't know it's here.

Opening the letter, I was shocked. The IRS said that the company owned payroll taxes on the paychecks for the last three months that I've been here, and since we hadn't paid when we were supposed to, we now owe penalties and interest. Apparently, payroll taxes are due within three business days of cutting payroll checks, and the IRS considers that money "they're money." All I can say is…"WHOOPS!"

So now I have a dilemma. Do I show the boss the letter and have him cut the check right away? Or, do I just hide this letter and try to deal with it a little at a time, without the boss knowing? Obviously, the first choice comes with the unfortunate consequence of the boss coming to believe that I don't know how to do my job when I do (I mean – Seriously! It was one simple mistake). The latter choice means that he continues thinking I'm brilliant, and that the company is doing better in my hands…

Hmmmm…choices, choices.

Although, now that I think about it, I see a third option here. I could always continue to fill out the payroll tax forms, but instead of cutting the IRS checks, I could just take the payroll tax money and enter the taxes as "Paid" in the bookkeeping program. The boss will think that I'm paying the taxes, and I can make a little extra on the side. Then, if the IRS does ever come calling, I can just explain it away as, "the bookkeeping program must have made an error in calculating the payroll taxes." After all, it's not like the boss would expect me to stay on top of all the interest rates.

And how often does the IRS come calling? I mean, Really?

You know what they say, "Ignorance is bliss."

Keeping a Clean Bill of Health with the IRS

I've often told my clients, "The IRS is an unforgiving mistress." Would this piss the IRS off to hear? Sure…but I think they would rather keep their intimidating reputation than have people painting them as sweet and kind.

The facts are these…The IRS considers themselves debt collectors for the people. The money that a business is supposed to pay does NOT belong to the business, but to the business's employees the moment those checks are cut (at least in the IRS's point of view). What that means is, they will NOT negotiate on when you can and cannot pay payroll taxes. You should pay it within three business days of the checks being cut, PERIOD. And if you ask employees to hold off on cashing their checks until you can get some money in the bank account, you could suffer fines as high as $25,000 per Employee Check. (Imagine it…your business is strapped for cash, and so you ask your employees to wait a week to cash their checks. Then you fire a bad employee. What will they do? They'll run to the IRS and report you, and BAM – bye, bye business.)

The point I'm dancing around here is that – YOU DON'T MESS WITH THE IRS! You – whether you're the bookkeeper or the business owner – need to make sure the taxes get paid on time. Since payments can now be made over the phone directly from a checking account, the business owner will likely never see a payroll tax check to cut. That means, the business owner needs to check up on their bookkeeper and make sure the taxes were paid, or you could suffer huge fines.

To Make Sure the IRS Taxes are Being Paid

This step merely comes down to one thing yet again. Open your bank statements and look at it. You will probably see the payments listed near the top, detailed out as an EFTPS payment to the IRS. It's that simple. If you don't see the payments cut as often as payroll is cut, get it taken care of immediately.

One Last Note for Small Business Owners

The mistake of not paying the payroll taxes is VERY common with a lot of bookkeepers. The biggest reason is that many bookkeepers are office managers that were handed a company's check register and told to "take care of it." So, just because payroll taxes may not have been paid at your company, doesn't mean your bookkeeper is an embezzler. It could just mean that they aren't on top of everything they're supposed to be doing yet. Make sure your bookkeeper is on top of the IRS forms, and definitely talk to your accountant for help. That's an accountant's main job – to deal with the IRS.

Diary of a Bad, Bad Bookkeeper

Diary of a Bad, Bad Bookkeeper: (Day 200) - Why the Accountant Did NOT Catch Me

Dear Diary,

Let me just say – Whew! What a relief. Tax time is over and I got off scott-free.

You see, I was very concerned that when I handed over the business books to the accountant this year, I would be busted – caught – nailed to the wall. I was sure I'd be in Shawshank before long, and I was almost tempted to clean up my act – almost. I was sure I was cooked when the accountant called me a couple days ago and asked for the bookkeeping program's "Accountant backup." How could the accountant NOT see at an instant that I've been embezzling from the company for months now, especially when they have completely access to everything I've done?

But I got lucky.

Turns out, the accountant only wanted the backup of the program so that he could enter the usual accountant adjustments like depreciating the assets, updating interest balances, and adjusting the Cost of Goods Sold account. And thankfully, most of that information was updated from the reports that I created for the accountant's perusal.

Still, it was a long couple of days as I waited for the Accountant's copy to be returned.

And then the wait was over. The accountant copy was back and the accountant had praised me to the boss. He went so far as to say that I "kept a clean set of books."

The boss was so happy, he gave me a raise.

I never thought I'd say it – but I'm glad the accountant looked at the books. I can't wait until next year. I'm thinking, maybe I'll create a second set of books... just in case the accountant ever decides to look closer.

Why the Accountant Did NOT Catch the Embezzlement

This is a concern I hear from a lot of business owners that were embezzled from. Even more often, I hear business owners that have NOT been embezzled from telling me that they are NOT worried about embezzlement because "they have an accountant." Both types of business owners usually believe that when they hand over their books at the end of the year, the accountant is automatically going to look deeply between the lines and spot anything suspicious.

FINDING EMBEZZLEMENT IS NOT THE ACCOUNTANT'S JOB… *not unless they're asked*.

During tax time, accountants are bombarded with books from various businesses. They have a very limited amount of time to do everything from sending out tax forms to making adjustments to various accounts. In other words – tax time is an accountant's "busy season." They often have a preset list of actions to do with any business's books.

Another Example of Missed Embezzlement

Let me state this another way. Recently, I have been working with a non-profit branch of a company that reports their profits and losses to their "parent" company. Since the company is a non-profit branch (or chapter) and NOT a business that is run in the usual ways, this branch reports does NOT report directly to the IRS or an accountant. Instead, they are sent a questionnaire from the parent company that they have to fill out and send back to the parent company. They are not asked for any backup, which makes it even easier to steal from the branch.

Recently, when I reported to the parent company that I saw signs of embezzlement in this particular branch, the parent company said they would look into the financials. When they looked over the reports that the embezzler made up for the chapter, they reported no signs of embezzlement. They openly admitted that they had to have a closer look at the records and the bank statements in order to verify if there was embezzlement or not. And since the branch (chapter) is not required in the non-profit policies and procedures, the branch could very well go under if a closer look at the books is not performed immediately.

How to Catch this Kind of Embezzlement

The only way for an accountant to catch this type of embezzlement is to have the business owner actually ASK the accountant to look for embezzlement. If the accountant is not asked, they will not look closer. They will go through their preset list of actions and look no further. The other way is to have someone else – preferably another bookkeeper – look more closely at the reports and compare them to the bank statements.

Diary of a Bad, Bad Bookkeeper: (Day 216) - Men Suck!

Dear Diary,

Today was another, "Not so great day"…but this time it was one for the books.

Today, when I went to work, I wasn't feeling so hot. In fact, I ended up puking into my office trash can just as the boss walked in.

"Hey," he says to me, looking concerned. "You're sick? You shouldn't be here if you're sick. Go home!"

"She was sick yesterday too," the traitor receptionist chimed in from behind him. "She's been sick for a while."

"Have you been to a doctor?" the boss asked me.

"No. I don't need to go to the doctor, okay!" I snapped. "I'm fine."

"You're three shades of green," he countered. "You should definitely go home. You may have the flu. Or even worse, food poisoning. In fact, I insist you go home until you get better."

The receptionist gave me a triumphant smile from over his shoulder. The witch never liked me.

"I won't get better for another eight months, alright!" I bit out, my eyes narrowing at her.

The receptionist's eyes widened. She understood right away.

My boss didn't get it, of course. He never does. "Why do you say that? What happens in eight months?"

"That's when she has a baby," the receptionist chimed in.

The boss's eyes widened, his expression immediately going to my still-flat belly. "You're pregnant?"

"Yes, I am," I growled. And I don't know who the father is, I silently added. It was either my husband (who would be over the moon if he thought I was pregnant), or Ernie (the employee who had blackmailed me into looking the other way while he stole from the company…let's just say that things have progressed between us). If it's Ernie's baby…well, he'd probably be thrilled too.

Men Suck!

"That's fantastic!" the boss said.

You suck too!

Diary of a Bad, Bad Bookkeeper

His expression changed as he looked at me though. I could see the exact moment when he realized this was going to affect my place in the company sometime in the near future.

Heading him off, I said, "But you don't need to worry about me missing any work. I'm not much of a stay-at-home mom. I won't need more than a few days off from work when the time comes."

His face twisted. "Are you kidding? That's a very important time in a child's life. It's when they bond with their child. You'll want more than a few days off of work."

"You forget…I have two children already. There's no way on Earth I want to spend any more time with a child. Trust me. I'll be back for work fairly quickly."

"Oh don't be foolish," the receptionist chimed in. "You'll definitely want time off. And I know just the place to call to get a temp in here."

Did I mention I hate the receptionist?

"That sounds like a good idea," the boss said, smiling at her like she was brilliant. "Why don't you call them and see how much they cost." Turning back to me, he says, "And you don't worry about anything, Betty. When the time comes, your job will be here. We love having you here. You take all the time you need to bond with your baby. In the meantime, can I get you something? Are you hungry?"

I could feel my teeth grinding. "I'm fine."

"Well then, I guess I'll let you get back to work. You take it easy. And don't worry about the trash. I'll send Ernie in to empty that for you."

Then the boss left, shuffling the receptionist off with him.

So now I'm freaking out. Time off? I can't take time off. What if someone catches onto what I'm doing? What if the next bookkeeper is better than me? What am I going to do?

Why Skipping Vacations is a Warning Sign

While this article is a bit more of a dramatization then I usually go for, there is a point here. The point is, this is a warning sign:

Whenever a bookkeeper doesn't want to take a vacation, maternity leave, or even call in sick…it could be a warning sign.

You see…good bookkeepers aren't worried about people going through their offices, whether other staff or other bookkeepers. Good bookkeepers make themselves replaceable at all times (in my opinion). The best bookkeepers have nothing to hide or fear.

Embezzling bookkeepers, on the other hand, fear anyone going through their paperwork, their computer files, and sometimes even their filing cabinets. They fear being caught all the time. Taking time off for maternity leave or going on vacation is often when they get caught.

Instead, they spend as much time in the office as they can, protecting the terrible things they've done, as well as their secrets.

How to Know For Sure

As always, if you are concerned that your bookkeeper is embezzling from you, hire someone to look more closely at your books. Accountants do not do this unless asked. Virtual Bookkeepers or Independent Bookkeepers are an excellent source for looking for fraudulent activity.

Start by getting a backup of your bookkeeping program when your bookkeeper is not around, and send it to the hired auditor. Also get copies of your bank statements. These two things will help them get started looking for embezzlement. From there, they will either ask for copies of suspicious checks, credit card statements, receipts…and any number of things.

The key is…if you suspect, don't site blindly by. Take this as a warning sign and ask someone for help. It's better to spend a few hundred dollars hiring an auditor then to lose thousands and thousands to an embezzler.

Diary of a Bad, Bad Bookkeeper

Diary of a Not-So-Bad, Somewhat-Honest, "Better-Than-Betty" Bookkeeper

Diary of a Bad, Bad Bookkeeper

Diary of a Not-So-Bad, Somewhat-Honest, "Better-Than-Betty" Bookkeeper: (Day 7) – Oh Crap! What do I do?

Dear Diary,

What do I do? I've only been at this new job for a week now and I'm totally at a loss. I am temping at this small business because the previous bookkeeper went on maternity leave. I'm only supposed to be here for six weeks. How do I tell this really nice Small Business Owner that his previous bookkeeper was stealing from him. And not just a little bit – *oh no!* Just from a first quickie-audit, I can tell that she's stolen tens of thousands of dollars in the year or so that she was working here. I really do *not* want to be the messenger. You know what they always say about the messenger…

To make matters worse, the boss seems like a decent guy. One of the first things he said to me was, "My bookkeeper Betty is the sweetest and most loyal employee I've ever had. She really wanted to keep working even though she just had a baby – probably because company is in a bit of a tough financial situation at the moment. She's saved this company more than a hundred times from angry vendors. Heck, I had to force her to take leave. I don't know how we're going to make it around here without her."

How do I tell him that the reason the business is going through "a bit of a tough financial situation" is because his "oh so sweet" bookkeeper was actually embezzling from him?

How do I tell him that the business is on the verge of shutting their doors because of *her*? I mean, he obviously trusts her completely. I've only been there a week. Why would he trust me?

I should have quit the first day. I should have quit as soon as I got those three phone calls from those vendors saying they wouldn't let us take our job materials unless we paid cash. One was easy enough to explain away, but three?

I didn't want to believe it at first – I really didn't. But when the balance on the bank statement didn't match what was entered in QuickBooks, I knew something was wrong. So I quickly redid a few reconciliations to check, and sure enough, things were missing from the books. In the last few months alone, it's clear she stole almost $5,000. But it could even be more than that. I wouldn't really know unless I did a full audit on the books?

How could the owner not have caught on when it's that much money?

Do I tell the owner right away, or should I gather as much evidence as possible? *Sigh* What to do? What to do?

Beginning the Audit Process

As you can tell, this diary entry is a bit different than the previous entries. While all of the previous entries were about *Preventing* a Betty Bookkeeper from stealing from you, this entry is about beginning the process of uncovering the truth. Is your bookkeeper a Betty Bookkeeper? Or was a previous bookkeeper a Betty Bookkeeper? The only real way to know is to begin an audit.

Who Should Do the Audit:

Now obviously, you can hire an accountant to audit your books, but that can be a really expensive audit since accountants usually charge hundreds of dollars an hour. Instead, you should consider hiring a Freelance Bookkeeper to come in an audit your books. Freelance Bookkeepers (the ones who own their own businesses) have usually reached a level of speed and efficiency that most bookkeepers or office managers hired from the newspaper may not have reached. Their going rate is usually in the two digits per hour instead of the three digits per hour.

Now if that still is too much for you, the next best thing would be to hire someone from a temp agency to come in and redo your bookkeeping for the period which your Suspected Bookkeeper worked. It may take a couple months for them depending on the length of time the Suspected Bookkeeper worked, the number of transactions to enter and the skill level of the person you hired.

"But I only Suspect my Bookkeeper right now. What do I do if I just want to check?"

How to Do a Quickie Audit:

If the above is something you're thinking, then take heart. You can actually start with a "Quickie Audit" to help confirm or allay your suspicions.

But before you do anything, **MAKE SURE TO MAKE A BACKUP OF YOUR FILE AS IT IS RIGHT NOW**. As soon as you start making changes in your bookkeeping account, you start undoing "evidence." Make a backup and save it somewhere your "suspect" can't get to it (preferably on your home computer).

1. **Undo the Last Few Bank Reconciliations**: Now, if you have QuickBooks, a quickie audit is going to be fairly simple. You would go to "Bank" then "Reconciliations." Right away, a screen would pop up which asks which account you want to reconcile. Pick your bank account or credit card account, and then find the button or link that says "Undo Last Bank Reconciliation." You can click on that link as many times as you want and undo as many Bank Reconciliations as you need until you are at a place where you would like to start.

Pay attention as you do this. Some versions of QuickBooks will give you a list of checks, debits and deposits that were ***deleted*** during that period. If you see those items, write those amounts and reference numbers (i.e. check numbers) down before you click the "Undo Last Bank Reconciliation" button again. With some QuickBooks versions, this is the ONLY time you will see those numbers, and you *will* want them. They are transactions you need to look at more closely if you truly suspect your bookkeeper. Write them down on a piece of paper or do and save a screen capture. (You most likely won't be able to print those items otherwise.)

If you have a different bookkeeping program, look for the same "Undo Last Bank Statement" feature. Hopefully there is one. *If not, you may have to create a new set of books from scratch.*

2. **Get Out Your Bank Statements and Reconcile Your Account up to Date**: I know, I know... this is too simple. How could a reconciliation help with an audit? Simple. Once you're done with the bank reconciliations, you are going to have a leftover *printable* list of items that have NOT gone through the bank. They are items that you will want to hunt down and look at more closely.

An Easy Way to Reconcile: If your bookkeeper really did steal from you, there will not only be a list of items that you have to look up, but there will be items that were deleted from your bookkeeping program which are on your bank statements. You will most likely have to enter these items into your books in order to get your books to reconcile. **My trick at making this easy is to underline the missing items on the bank statements and then enter the items quickly into the bookkeeping program under a Vendor Named "Look at More Closely" or "???" and under a new category I like to call "Unknown Items".** By creating a single "vendor" and "Unknown Items" category to assign these items too, you will end up with another list of things to look at in one printable place and the amounts won't adjust the category balances you already have. Plus, this makes it a lot easier to find later as you find and fix those items.

Make sure to put in the reference numbers from the bank statements as you enter the missing items.

3. **Get Your Lists Together**: Once you've done the reconciliation, like I said, you will have three lists of transactions to begin hunting down. You should have the "Deleted Items" you saw before you started the reconciliation, your "Look at More Closely" Vendor, and your list of "Items Not Yet Reconciled." (If you don't have the first, don't worry. It's the second two which are the most important.) While you're at it, print out your Reconciliation <u>***Detail***</u> (not the Summary) from your bookkeeping program as well. This will give you names, dates, and transaction numbers.

4. **Begin the Hunt**: Next, you want to get all copies of checks that you have on hand. Organize them in ascending order by check number. While this is a time-consuming pain-in-the-a** to do, it really is your best and fastest option in doing a quickie audit.

If you have a printout of all your checks from the bank, consider yourself lucky. This is an easier way to compare your checks to your statements and your lists.

Don't forget to look closely at the checks. Is it your signature on every check? Do you know every business and person who cashed one of your checks? Any name that is suspicious, mark that also for more research later.

5. **Compare**: With your checks in order, begin the comparison. Match your checks to the reconciliation details. If the check doesn't match the Reconciliation Detail list, either set it aside into a "Doesn't Match"

pile or tag the check with a post it note that hangs off the end of the check. Either way will help you later when re-entering those items into your bookkeeping program.

Any checks that are missing, you will have to get from the bank. In other words, let's say that your bank statement says a check was cashed for a certain amount, but you don't have the check to verify it. Then, you will need to contact the bank and see if you can look at a copy of it. Luckily, most banks these days allow you to see a copy of the bank when you login to your bank account online. If your bank doesn't have this feature, you may have to pay a fee to see each check. This can be expensive, so you may want to start with the few with the highest balances. After all, the bank charges aren't about the price of the check but the printing itself.

You may notice that some of the check numbers from your "Not Yet Reconciled" list have already gone through the bank for different amounts. Obviously, that's a bad sign. That means it's a "duplicate" entry, or it is an entry that was made to replace another entry. Obviously, items that have not gone through the bank actually might still be sitting somewhere un-cashed, so make sure you don't jump to conclusions just because you have a list of Unreconciled Items. Just know that those items are items that need more research.

And that's it. That is how you do a Quickie Audit. It will work on pretty much any checking account and is the fastest way to look for suspicious activity. This method will also work on credit card accounts.

Now as I've detailed out in this eBook, there are plenty of other ways for a bookkeeper or even an employee to steal from you, but the checking account and credit cards are the easiest and most tempting way for a bookkeeper to steal from a business. So most likely, if your bookkeeper really is stealing, you will find something here.

If you go through all of this, but still feel something is wrong, then you really should hire an expert. After all, they will most likely have to recreate the books back from the beginning in order to really find how bad your bookkeeper could be.

Finally, don't jump to conclusions just because you find suspicious activity. Ask your accountant or a Freelance Bookkeeper to take a second look first.

Getting Your Money Back:

Are you ready for something *really* scary? If not, don't read this part…

Still here? Okay, here goes.

From the research I've done, most embezzlers *do not* serve even one year in prison for their crimes.

Even worse, if an embezzler is caught, they often cut a deal with the victim to pay back a certain portion of the money and then their crime is never reported. This leaves them "on the street" to go and do this to another business.

In all honesty, you probably won't get all of your money back. Or, the embezzler may choose a short stint in prison over paying back a truly astronomical amount of money. If this is the case for you, you only have a few options:

1. **Take them to court anyway and try to get your money back.** A court judgment is actionable. If the person doesn't pay you back within a certain time period, you can often garnish their wages from their next judgment.

2. **Make a Settlement with them to get whatever you can get back**. Again, you probably won't get all of it since most likely, they've been happily spending it as they've been stealing it from you. However, they will most likely have something left. Take everything you can get, including their car if they have one. Some embezzlers will agree if it means that you won't press charges.

3. **Get Revenge**: (*This is a last resort type of situation. If you do it, make sure you wait until **after** the court judgment or after you have tried to settle with them. If you do it before, you may lose a chance at getting any money back.*) If they refuse to pay you, then press charges and do everything you can to make them go to jail. It will make it that much harder for them to do to someone else. Once you have your court judgment or your settlement **in your hand,** *then and only then,* 1099 their a**. Send them a 1099 for the amount they got away with. When the IRS gets a copy of that person's 1099, they will go and do their own audit of that person's finances. They will even tax them for the stolen income. While it may not be as satisfying as sending them to jail for the rest of their lives, having the IRS breathing down your neck for an unknown period is almost as scary as prison.

Good luck.

Diary of a Bad, Bad Bookkeeper

Did You Like this Book?

Want a Printable PDF Version for free?

I'll trade you for it. I am offering two different ways to get the printable version for free.

1) **Review the book on Amazon, Barnes & Noble, GoodReads or even Smashwords.** Every book review helps an author whether the review is good or bad. If you would give the book an honest review, I would be super appreciative. Here are the shortcut addresses:

   - www.OneHourBookkeeper.com/DiaryOnAmazon
   - www.OneHourBookkeeper.com/DiaryOnBarnes
   - www.OneHourBookkeeper.com/DiaryOnGoodreads
   - www.OneHourBookkeeper.com/DiaryOnSmashwords

   Then just email me at IReviewedTheDiary@OneHourBookkeeper.com and I will send you a link where you can download the printable version.

   Or you can:

2) **Tell Me Your Embezzlement Stories.** I would like to create a sequel to The Diary of a Bad, Bad Bookkeeper, but I have already written down every scam I can think of. If you know of a scam I have missed, or something happened that you would like to learn how to prevent, send me your story at

Diary of a Bad, Bad Bookkeeper

ForTheNextDiary@OneHourBookkeeper.com and I will send you the link to the downloadable version.

Thank you for reading The Diary of a Bad, Bad Bookkeeper. If you would like to read more of my business, bookkeeping or blogging advice, visit my website at www.OneHourBookkeeper.com. Or if you have any questions, feel free to email me at ETBarton@OneHourBookkeeper.com.

Also, if you would like to join my email newsletter and get tips on bookkeeping, business, or blogging, then simply shoot an email to:

Newsletter@OneHourBookkeeper.com.

Be sure to check your email inbox and confirm that you want to be on the list. (Your email will never be sold, and I do not believe in spamming.)

Other Products by E.T. Barton or the OneHourBookkeeper.com website:

THE ONE HOUR BOOKKEEPING METHOD: How To Do Your Books In One Hour Or Less

HOW TO START A LUCRATIVE VIRTUAL BOOKKEEPING BUSINESS: A Step-by-Step Guide to Working Less and Making More in the Bookkeeping Industry

HOW TO DO A YEAR'S WORTH OF BOOKKEEPING IN ONE DAY

A Step-by-Step Guide for Small Businesses

10 WAYS TO SAVE MONEY ON BOOKKEEPING & ACCOUNTING

DIARY OF A BAD, BAD BOOKKEEPER

A Cautionary Embezzlement Tale

for Small Business Owners Everywhere

HOW TO TWITTER ON AUTO-PILOT

An Internet Marketing Guide for

Business Owners and Entrepreneurs

All Available at:

www.OneHourBookkeeper.com

www.ingramcontent.com/pod-product-compliance
Lightning Source LLC
Chambersburg PA
CBHW061514180526
45171CB00001B/181